The Forgotten Garden

Written by Maisie Chan

Illustrated by Miriam Serafin

Collins

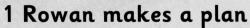

1 Rowan makes a plan

Rowan and his mum spotted Mrs Lee in
the porch of her bungalow.

She had been living alone for years.

"Hello!" Mrs Lee said. "I'm going to hospital for a week. I was hoping you might feed my cat, Flo, when I am away?"

"No problem," said Rowan.

The next day, Rowan's mum sent him to fill up
Flo's bowl.

But when he stepped into the back garden, he was shocked by how overgrown it was.

He rushed back home.
"Mum, we have got to help!" Rowan said.
"Mrs Lee cannot get out into her garden.
The weeds are so high!"

2 Friends dig in

Rowan started by mowing.

Then he weeded with a hoe.

Next he shifted a rock the size of a boulder out of an overgrown flowerbed.

It was no surprise Mrs Lee was struggling with the garden. There was too much for Rowan to do on his own.

He needed extra hands to help.

Rowan sipped his drink then had a brainwave!
He rang his friends from the gardening club
at school.

They arrived the next morning, willing and eager.

Rowan showed his friends the plan. He told them what they had to do.

They dug a long shallow hole down the side and sowed a row of flowers.

Rowan and his mum went to the shops and chose ten pots of red and yellow roses.

Rowan and his friends put the roses under Mrs Lee's back window.

At the end of the week, Mrs Lee arrived home.
She was glad to be back.

Rowan and his mum helped her with her bags.

3 Back home

They took her out to the garden. "Don't peek,"
Rowan said. "We hope you like it!"

"I love a surprise," Mrs Lee said.

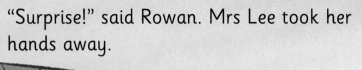

"Surprise!" said Rowan. Mrs Lee took her
hands away.

The garden was stunning. Bees buzzed in lilac lavender, green shrubs glowed with bright flowers.

Mrs Lee gazed at the garden for a long time.
A tear fell down her cheek.

Rowan's shoulders slumped. "What's the matter?" he said.

"It's … perfect!" Mrs Lee said.

"I haven't been gardening for so long. I didn't like to come out. Now I can spend lots of time in my fantastic garden."

Mrs Lee's garden

After reading

Letters and Sounds: Phase 5
Word count: 379
Focus phonemes: /ai/ ay, a-e, ey /ee/ ea /igh/ i-e, i /oa/ o, oe, ow, oul, o-e
Common exception words: of, to, the, into, by, put, are, my, she, we, be, said, have, do, when, what, school, Mrs, friends, there, out, was, you, asked, he, some, love, come
Curriculum links: Science: Plants; PSHE: Communities
National Curriculum learning objectives: Reading/word reading: read accurately by blending the sounds in words that contain the graphemes taught so far, especially recognising alternative sounds for graphemes; Reading/comprehension (KS2): understand what they read, in books they can read independently, by checking that the text makes sense to them, discussing their understanding and explaining the meaning of words in context; making inferences on the basis of what is being said and done; predicting what might happen on the basis of what has been read so far

Developing fluency

- Your child may enjoy hearing you read the book.
- Take turns to read a page. Ask your child to use different voices for the narrator, Rowan and Mrs Lee.

Phonic practice

- Focus on the different spellings of the sound /oa/. Ask your child to sound out the following, and identify what letters make the /oa/ sound:
  bungalow (*ow*)   roses (*o-e*)   going (*o*)   hoe (*oe*)
- Challenge your child to sound out these words. Remind them that different sounds may be written with the same letters.
  overgrown   bowl   flowers   showed

Extending vocabulary

- On page 7, the garden is **overgrown**. Ask your child to think of a word or phrase with a similar meaning to **overgrown**. (e.g. *wild*, *untidy*)
- Together, think of words or phrases that have a similar meaning to these:
  Page 15: eager (e.g. *keen*)   page 23: love (e.g. *adore*)
  page 29: fantastic (e.g. *amazing*)